I Can Read About
Dinosaurs

Written by John Howard • Illustrated by Christopher Santoro

Consultant: Dr. Niles Eldredge, Curator
Department of Invertebrates, American Museum of Natural History

Troll Associates

Library of Congress Cataloging-in-Publication Data
Howard, John, (date)
        I can read about dinosaurs / written by John Howard ;
illustrated by Christopher Santoro ; consultant, Niles Eldredge.
            p.   cm.
        ISBN 0-8167-3638-3 (lib. bdg.). — ISBN 0-8167-3639-1 (pb.)
        1. Dinosaurs—Juvenile literature.   [1. Dinosaurs.]
I. Santoro, Christopher, ill.   II. Title.
QE862.D5H69   1996
567.9'1—dc20   95-5945

Plateosaurus

Millions of years ago, when much of the world was warm and
swampy, strange-looking creatures called dinosaurs roamed the earth.

Coelophysis

The early dinosaurs were not very big.

But slowly, over many years, they grew larger and larger.

Camarasaurus

Brachiosaurus

One of the biggest dinosaurs of all was Brachiosaurus (BRAK-ee-uh-sawr-us). It was about 75 feet (23 meters) long and probably stood about 39 feet (12 meters) tall.

Apatosaurus (ah-PAT-uh-sawr-us) was almost as large as Brachiosaurus. This dinosaur had a very long neck and tail and was about 70 feet (22 meters) long.

Apatosaurus

Diplodocus

One of the longest dinosaurs was Diplodocus (dih-PLOD-uh-kus). It grew to be 88 feet (27 meters) long.

Many of these dinosaurs were plant-eaters. They had small, rounded teeth and spent much of their time hunting for berries, seeds, ferns, and leaves.

These plant-eating dinosaurs were gentle creatures.

But other dinosaurs were not gentle. They were fierce
meat-eaters with sharp, pointed teeth. They hunted
other dinosaurs and smaller
animals for food.

Deinonychus

Plant-eaters sometimes had to hide
from the meat-eaters. Some plant-eaters
fled to the water to escape their enemies.

Tenontosaurus

Allosaurus

Stegosaurus

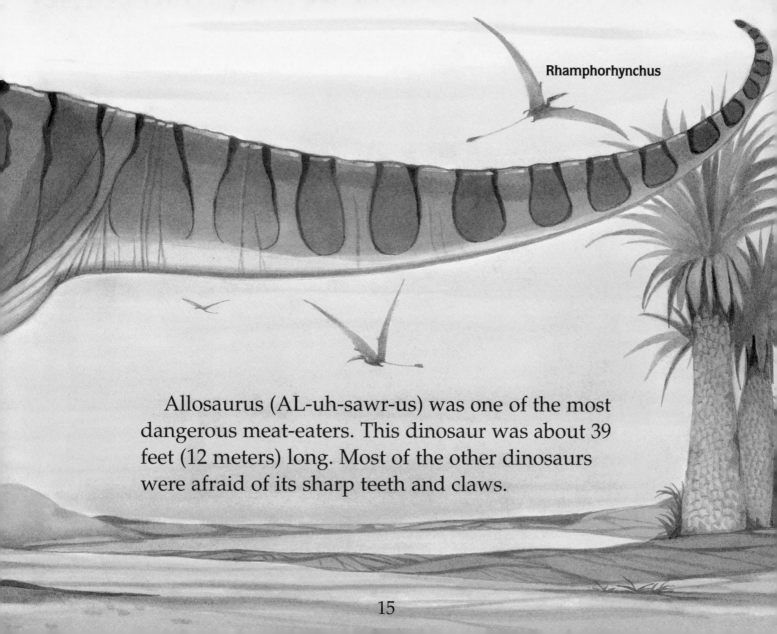

Rhamphorhynchus

Allosaurus (AL-uh-sawr-us) was one of the most dangerous meat-eaters. This dinosaur was about 39 feet (12 meters) long. Most of the other dinosaurs were afraid of its sharp teeth and claws.

Some plant-eaters had armor for protection. When Stegosaurus (STEG-uh-sawr-us) swung its spiked tail, Allosaurus learned to leave Stegosaurus alone.

Stegosaurus

Allosaurus

Tyrannosaurus

After many years, Allosaurus died out. But a bigger and more terrible giant, called Tyrannosaurus (tye-RAN-uh-sawr-us), took its place. Tyrannosaurus was about 49 feet (15 meters) long. Its sharp teeth could be up to 7 inches (18 centimeters) long!

Anatosaurus (ah-NAT-uh-sawr-us) had a lot of very small teeth that it used to grind up plants. Anatosaurus's duck-billed mouth was very useful for gathering food.

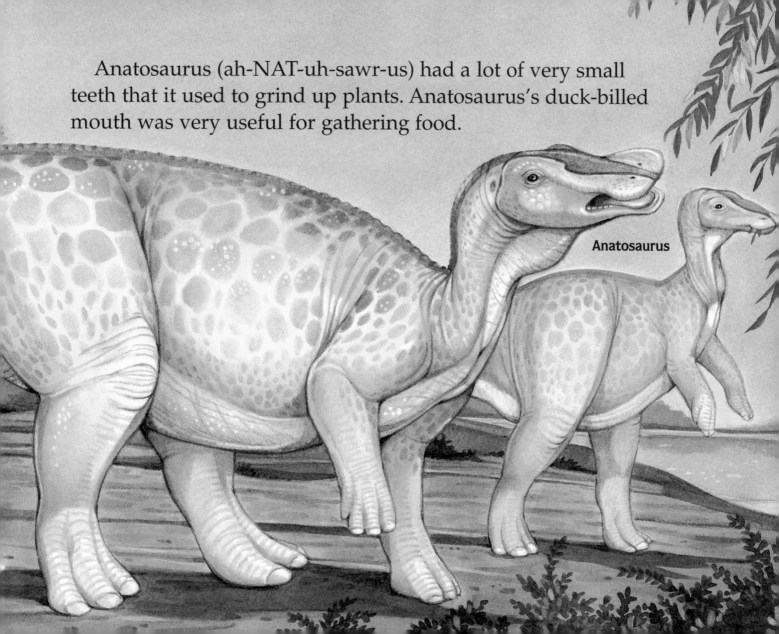

Anatosaurus

Meat-eaters could usually run much faster than plant-eaters. If Tyrannosaurus caught Anatosaurus before it could escape to the water...

Tyrannosaurus

Anatosaurus

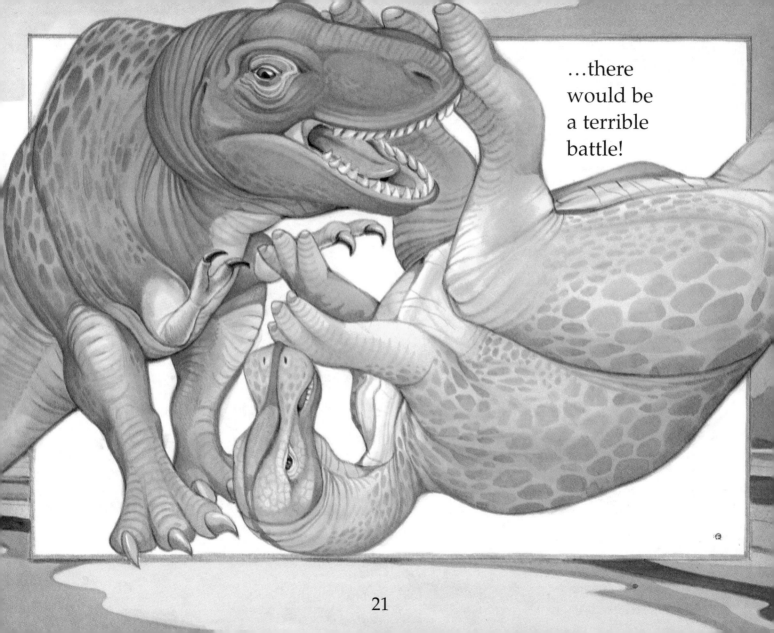

...there would be a terrible battle!

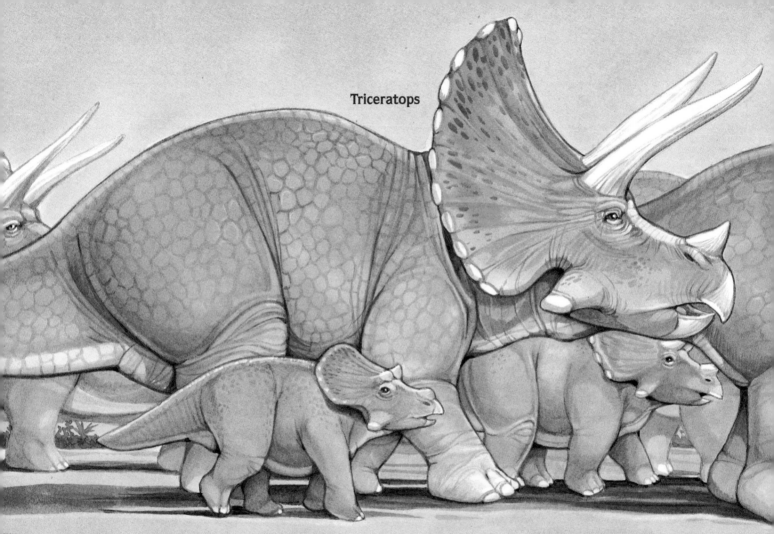

Triceratops

Some plant-eaters could fight mighty Tyrannosaurus. One of these was Triceratops (try-SAIR-uh-tops).

Tyrannosaurus

Triceratops could defend itself very well with its long, pointed horns and the bony shield behind its head.

23

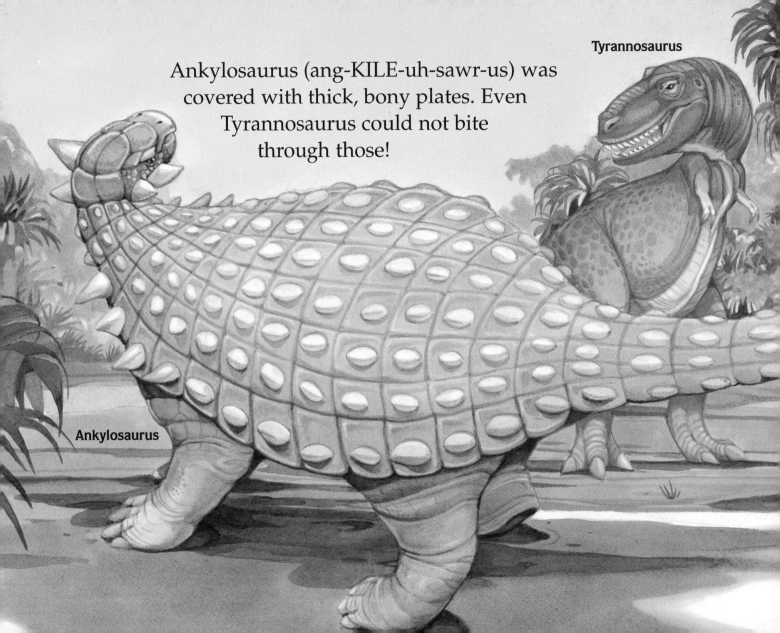

Ankylosaurus (ang-KILE-uh-sawr-us) was covered with thick, bony plates. Even Tyrannosaurus could not bite through those!

Tyrannosaurus

Ankylosaurus

Even though these dinosaurs were large, their small brains were about the size of a kitten's.

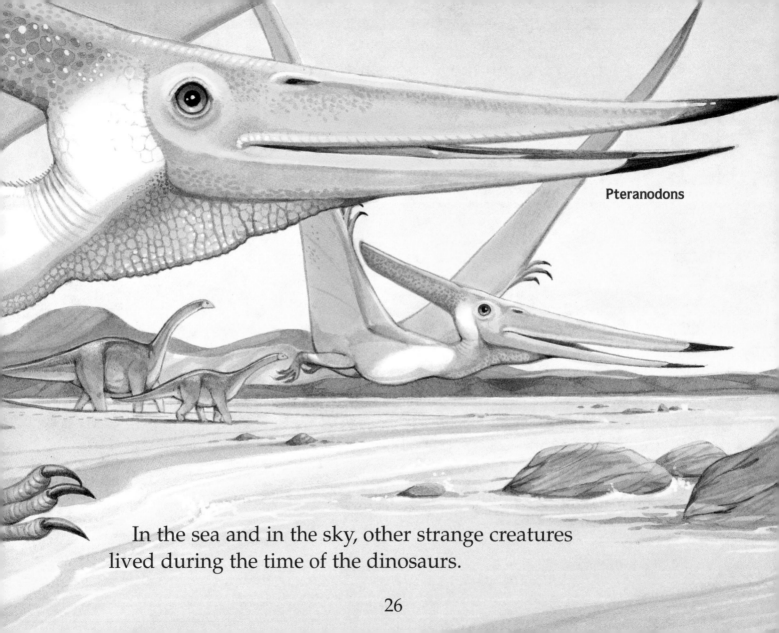

Pteranodons

In the sea and in the sky, other strange creatures lived during the time of the dinosaurs.

The creatures of the sky had leathery or
scaly skin instead of feathers. These meat-
eaters could swoop down to catch
smaller animals.

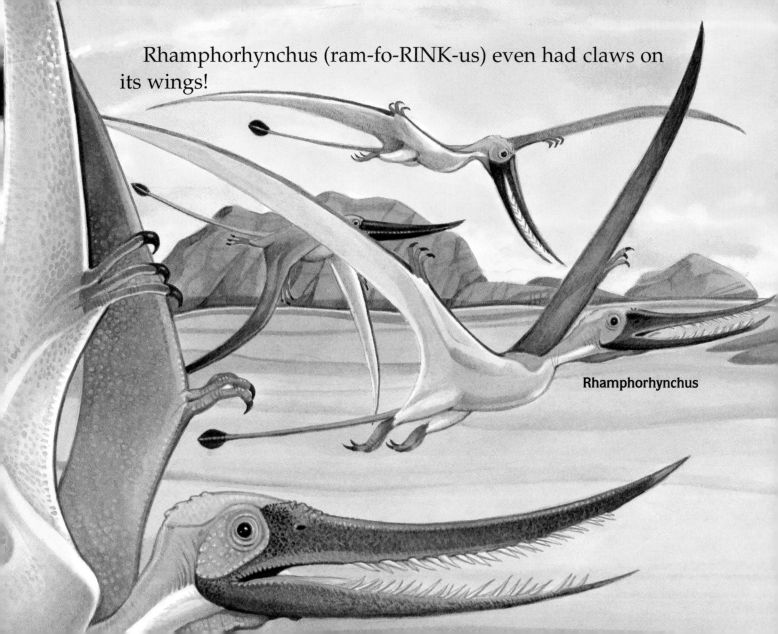

Rhamphorhynchus (ram-fo-RINK-us) even had claws on its wings!

Rhamphorhynchus

Some of the large creatures living in the sea looked like sea serpents. Elasmosaurus (ee-LAZ-mo-sawr-us) sometimes grew to be 50 feet (15 meters) long.

Elasmosaurus

Tyrannosaurus

After living for more than 100 million years, dinosaurs began to die out. Finally, they became extinct and vanished from the face of the earth.

No one is sure why the dinosaurs died. Some scientists think that a giant meteorite may have crashed into the earth. Perhaps the crash raised large clouds of dust that blocked out the sun for a long time.

Triceratops

The plants and animals that the dinosaurs ate could not live without the sun. The dinosaurs probably could not adapt to these and other changes, and may have died as a result.

When the dinosaurs disappeared, other animals called mammals began to take their places.

Opossum

Wooly mammoth

The mammals were small at first. After the dinosaurs had vanished, they started to grow and change.

Eohippus (EE-o-HIP-us) was the size of a fox.

Mesohippus (MES-o-HIP-us) was the size of a sheep.

Pliohippus (PLY-o-HIP-us) was the size of a donkey.

Equus (EH-qwus) was the size of a domestic horse.

Merychippus (MARE-ee-KIP-us) was the size of a small Shetland pony.

35

Mammoth

Among the biggest
mammals were the
mammoth...

...and its close cousin, the mastodon.
Both of these animals were related to elephants.

Mastodon

One of the fiercest mammals was the saber-toothed tiger.
Even the mammoths were afraid of its long teeth.

Wooly mammoth

Saber-toothed tiger

Soon after humans appeared on the earth, most of these early mammals died out. This might have happened because the weather turned colder again, and there was not enough food.

Perhaps these mammals were hunted down by early humans.

Today you can see the skeletons of dinosaurs and early mammals in museums.

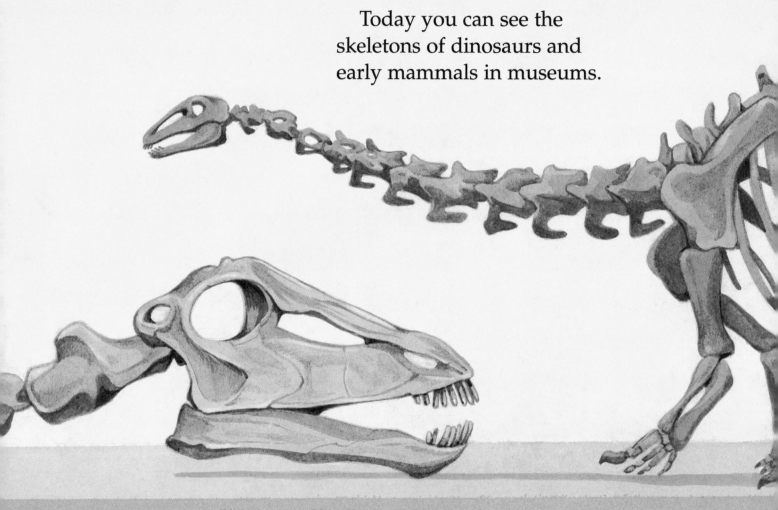

Diplodocus — Plant-Eater

There you can see the differences between the teeth and jaws of a meat-eating dinosaur and a plant-eating dinosaur.

Allosaurus — Meat-Eater

43

Scientists have learned much about dinosaurs and other animals from bones and impressions discovered in rocks. These are called fossils. New fossils are still being found all over the world, and new discoveries about dinosaurs are being made all the time.

Recently, scientists have discovered that the birds we see today may be related to dinosaurs! Scientists have found fossils of a bird called Archaeopteryx (ar-kee-OP-ter-ix). It lived with the dinosaurs about 150 million years ago. It had feathers and wings, like modern birds. But Archaeopteryx also looked like a dinosaur and shared some dinosaur features, such as teeth, clawed fingers, and a flexible neck.

Archaeopteryx

Rhamphorhynchus

Apatosaurus

Fossils may teach us more about the dinosaurs and why they disappeared. They may even tell us about other prehistoric animals that have not been discovered yet.